EDUCATION LIBRARY SERVICE

Browning Way
Woodford Park Industrial Estate
Winsford
Cheshire CW7 2JN

Phone: 01606 592551/557126
Fax: 01606 861412
www.cheshire.gov.uk/els/home.htm

9.99

KT-405-568

TEN[10]

THE POWER OF TEN [10]

TEN PRODUCTS BY TEN BRITISH PRODUCT DESIGNERS
BY DAVID REDHEAD

CHESHIRE LIBRARIES

2 9 MAR 2003

LAURENCE KING

Hard

1. Modelling
2. New product development
3. Styling
4. Product graphics

Soft

1. Branding
2. CAD skills
3. Graphic user interface

Production management

New start up initiatives

Own product

Website design

Corporate Identity

Trendspotting
and forecasting

Qualitative market research

introduction07

What a difference a decade makes. Ten years ago, even the more design-conscious members of the British public would have been pushed to explain what a product designer did for a living let alone to actually name one.

Opposite product designers are increasingly diversifying beyond their traditional specialism in 'hard' skills to embrace the 'soft' aspects of design such as trendspotting, website design and branding.

But now that furniture has established itself as 'the new fashion', suddenly product design is almost sexy. In 21st century Britain, nitty gritty designers of everyday things are becoming the stuff of which gushing Sunday supplements and fashionable interiors magazine profiles are made. Vacuum cleaner designer-entrepreneur James Dyson is a household name, while Richard Seymour and Dick Powell have emerged as design's TV troubleshooting answer to Sir John Harvey-Jones thanks to the success of programmes such as *Designs on Your...*

As you might expect, the rising profile of the British product designer has been matched by increased prosperity for the product design industry. The UK trade magazine *Design Week* reported in July 1998 that the number of product designers in the UK had doubled in the past five years and that similar growth was likely to continue. According to the same magazine's annual industry survey in March 1999, four of the world's top ten product design consultancies were British.*

The new growth in design-consciousness notwithstanding, the progress made by product designers might seem to have been achieved against the odds. The influential economist Charles Leadbeater has argued that products have little part to play in the future of the 'advanced economy'. Forward thinkers, argues Leadbeater, should be focusing on the 'software' of IT, knowledge and service

* The four British companies in *Design Week*'s March 2000 global product design top ten were Cambridge Consultants, Fitch, Seymour Powell and PSD.

** 'Innovation has to be established as a deep value in business that is as deeply systematic as quality or efficiency.' Gary Hamel, Chairman of Strategos, *Design*, Winter 1998–99

industries if they are to prosper.

It's a fair point. Even if they do actually make something tangible, today's global corporations now think twice about taking on something as risky as managing the production of their own brands, if they can avoid it. They would rather 'outsource' the making to locations where products are cheap to make and assemble – probably to somewhere in the 'developing world'. 'The people who are manufacturers are only nominally so. They are just the people who bring out the ads,' argues Adam White of Factory. 'They just want to check the materials and the specification; they don't want the hassle of making the thing themselves.'

Cheeringly, the last decade has witnessed the emergence of a new spirit of manufacturing enterprise in Britain. James Dyson's successful reinvention of the vacuum cleaner has sparked a mini-explosion of new product ideas in the UK ranging from prams to Martin Myerscough's TKO-designed washing machine (see page 20). Even so, it is not really possible to put down the new prominence of

British product designers to a national manufacturing renaissance.

So how is it, you might wonder, that product designers are managing to buck what might appear to be a declining trend? Their new prominence clearly owes something to a shift in attitudes in business thinking. In the early 1990s, business opinion formers were full of the virtues of downsizing, cost-cutting and efficiency. Yet as competition has continued to intensify in the global market over the past decade, price has come to be seen as a less vital selling point than distinctiveness. And while hi-tech stocks may have caught a cold over the past year, design and innovation are still the new buzzwords of business thinkers from Tom Peters to Gary Hamel. **

Another factor that has boosted the currency of product design is the rise of brand culture. To the largely uninitiated British public of the 1980s, design seemed a mysterious unknown quantity, but in a millennial world in which we all intuitively grasp the rules of branding and corporate identity it has become obvious that manufacturers can no longer hope to turn

We were mistrusted by both sides so it's not really surprising that we were the designers who fell into the cracks.

Jim Fullalove director, Therefore

their fortunes around merely by repackaging or restyling a product. 'There was a time when graphic designers did type and product designers did toasters but the definition of a product has become much more holistic,' says Steve Hughes of PSD. 'Now people are recognising that the brand is the product and the product is the brand.'

For a profession sometimes tempted to think of itself as the creative world's unfairly marginalised poor relation, the new recognition of their skills in business circles naturally represents an experience to savour. It might seem odd that product design consultants have always been the smallest fee earners in the industry but they have been fighting a rearguard battle against manufacturing decline for years. Thanks to the high cost of 'tooling' for production, redesigning a product has often been seen as the option of last resort by potential clients.

Even in-house product designers were often overlooked by decision makers at boardroom level and were considered suspiciously arty by their production and engineering colleagues. 'Manufacturers

don't like a risk they can't understand or quantify and coming up with a brand new product design is much riskier than copying something or just changing the packaging,' says Jim Fullalove of Therefore design consultants. 'We were mistrusted by both sides so it's not really surprising that we were the designers who fell into the cracks.'

Inevitably perhaps, their embattled status forged a mentality among product specialists. 'I think there's often a determination about product designers that says "we'll deliver a good result whether people care or not",' says Jim Fullalove. 'It's partly a consequence of being ignored.'

Bulldog spirit or bloody-mindedness, on balance the siege mentality has probably been good for product designers, breeding a resilience that has stood them in good stead. Unlike their colleagues in retail, furniture and graphic design, product designers never really made it big in the design boom of the 1980s and never succumbed to the hubris which overcame many of their peers during the so-called 'designer decade'. While more glamorous colleagues in, say, retail design had over-

Now people are recognising that the brand is the product and the product is the brand.

Steve Hughes director, PSD

expanded and were ill-prepared for the shakeout which followed in the wake of Black Monday in 1989, product designers stayed small and evolved more slowly.

A dozen years after the crash, it is also clear that they have made a virtue of versatility. 'Products' today encompasses not just the hardware of consumer durables but vehicles, interiors, marketing devices and a whole series of services that underpin a brand from websites through market research to forecasting. 'It's impossible to be a product design company in the traditional sense any more,' says Andy Davey of TKO. 'We're doing the softer bits that connect the product with the consumer as well.' Adam White of Factory agrees: 'Being a product designer might mean anticipating the future, inventing things, supporting the brand, communicating a product's benefits to the consumer and managing the process of getting something made,' he says. 'It now encompasses everything from new toasters to new media.'

The character of clients who require design input at the beginning of the 21st century has changed almost as much as the nature of the skills required of designers. Product designers are still working for traditional British manufacturers that have constituted their bread and butter clients over the past 20 years: manufacturers of medical products, hi-fi systems, toys and computer hardware, for example. But, as the work in this book illustrates, they are also striking out into unfamiliar territory, taking on commissions from companies – among them Sky Broadcasting and Virgin Trains – who would probably not have been commissioning products even five years ago, if they existed at all.

The role of product design in some of these instances may be to give weight to high-profile marketing campaigns for those with less tangible 'products'. As the battle for transatlantic custom has hotted up among airline companies over the past few years, it seemed at times as if every top UK product design consultancy was creating a new seat for sleeping in, like Tangerine's airborne bed for British Airways (page 51), while companies such as Priestman Goode progressed to designing the whole interiors of planes, boats and trains (page 26).

'In the future it won't be enough to change
your strategy or to reinvent your industry.
You're going to have to do both.'
Gary Hamel, *Design,* Winter 1998–99

Meanwhile, Sky Broadcasting has
produced over five million of the distinctive
remote control devices designed by Frazer
Designers in the hope of reinventing its
image (see page 62). As Stephen Frazer
points out: 'Sky's customers didn't really
have anything that represented the
company. The remote uses the terms of
product design but its prime function is to
establish Sky as the official gatekeeper of
digital TV.'

The moral perhaps is that even the
pioneers of 'thin air economics' have a use
for corporate symbols that are substantial
and solid enough to hold in the palm of your
hand. It is an irony of the age that while
there may be fewer products emerging
from British factories today, business's
brand love affair has seen some product
designers achieve the sort of status that
they could only have dreamt of in British
manufacturing's golden age.

It is, for example, less common for
product designers to deal with lowly
product managers as once they did.
Instead, companies like those whose work
is shown here are regularly consulted by
boardroom level decision makers and their
input is as likely to consist of strategic ideas
and blue sky visions of the future as it is of
more conventional product concepts.
'What we do feels closer to management
consultancy than it did 20 years ago,'
says Ben Fether of FM Design. 'Designers
are emerging as business visionaries. We
open up clients' eyes to what a company
might be capable of.'

But if British product designers are taking
on new responsibilities as trendspotters,
production managers and marketing and
brand experts, the old ambition that first
brought them into product design – the
desire to create mass-market products in
their thousands and millions – still has an
important place in their hearts.

In this sense, what most catches the
imagination about the current generation
of product designers is that some are still
willing to defy the Jeremiahs by setting up
in manufacturing themselves. Product
designers taking up the making gauntlet
include Priestman Goode which is already
creating and making its own products
alongside more conventional design

If you don't want things to be spoiled in the making then doing it yourself is the obvious option open to you.

Nigel Goode director, Priestman Goode

commissions and which can point to successes including an upmarket radiator and a baby's changing mat that is sold through Mothercare. 'If you don't want things to be spoiled in the making then doing it yourself is the obvious option open to you,' says Nigel Goode. 'It is about empowering ourselves.'

The response of IDEO's American arm to the enterprise culture of Silicon Valley illustrates what empowerment might mean to product designers in the future. IDEO has already created a digital camera as an accessory for the Handspring hand-held computer it designed (page 39) and recently set up a manufacturing arm to explore other production possibilities.

Such creative partnerships may yet allow product designers to get a firmer foothold in manufacturing. Indeed, if the progress achieved in recent years by Cambridge Consultants Limited (CCL), the biggest company on Britain's product design scene, is anything to go by, an adventurous blend of collaboration and entrepreneurship may offer a potent blueprint for growth in the technologically-driven 21st century economy. Always a developer of its own new products as well as a designer of others, Cambridge Consultants is continuing to flourish both as a consultant and as an innovation hot house in its own right. Fresh from its success in creating the round tea bag for Tetley a year or two ago, the company's latest speculative product is a toaster which never burns the bread. Its latest spin-off company – Inca Digital Printers which was recently launched with £2.6 million worth of venture capital in which the company will retain a 15 per cent stake – is a typical addition to a burgeoning collection of profitable spin-offs for the printing industry.

At the moment, however, it is only fair to acknowledge that IDEO and Cambridge Consultants (whose work is not shown in this book) could hardly be described as typical. For all their imagination, Britain's product designers still remain minnows by comparison to CCL (which has a turnover of £27 million) or design's brand giants such as Interbrand Newell and Sorrell. Of the ten consultancies whose work is shown in this book only two can boast a turnover of more than £2 million per year or a staff much bigger than 30.

Even so, while total 'empowerment' remains a distant grail, the willingness of product designers to exploit new technologies and production techniques, to think laterally and to reinvent themselves for the modern world is likely to make them attractive both as consultants and partners for the sort of enterprising manufacturing and service companies that are likely to prosper in the New Economy. As the strategy guru Gary Hamel wrote a year or two ago: 'In the future it won't be enough to change your strategy or to reinvent your industry. You're going to have to do both.' It's a lesson that Britain's product designers already appear to have learned.

factory15

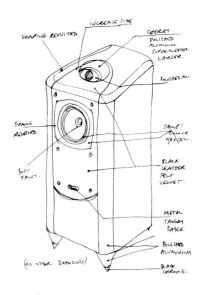

The sketch is annotated with the following handwritten labels: SHAPING REVISITED, INCREASE SIZE, CHERRY, POLISHED ALUMINIUM SUPER TWEETER LARGER, POLISHED ALU, FRAME ROUND, SAME COLOUR NEXT EL, SOFT PAINT, BLACK LEATHER FELT VELVET, METAL TANNOY BADGE, POLISHED ALUMINIUM, (NO OTHER BRANDING), BLACK CHROME.

Out of the box

Sound not style has sustained the market success of Scottish speaker manufacturer Tannoy. But now the company is rethinking its attitude to styling.

Opposite there was a time when all speakers seemed to share the same black and boxy form but the growth in design consciousness in lifestyle products has even penetrated the male-dominated and conservative British hi-fi market.
Top right the trapezoid form of the new Tannoy range is meticulously detailed.

There are many small British speaker manufacturers catering for the demanding ears of big-spending hi-fi connoisseurs. Thanks both to the skills of their acoustic engineers and their willingness to rebuild their products from the ground up, British brands like Mission, Wharfedale and Rogers have sustained an upmarket niche alongside brands like Bang & Olufsen in global markets as well as a cult following in the Far East.

Oddly, however, the rhythmic clarity and acuity with which British speakers are often associated has rarely been matched by the sharpness of their looks. Many companies seemed to view the very notion of visual styling with suspicion. Until recently the average speaker still looked very similar: oblong, boxy and plain, covered in black-stained ash veneer.

Until recently, the Glasgow-based company Tannoy – once a renowned maker of PA systems but now a speaker specialist – could have been counted among the visual neo-Luddites. Great as it sounded, for instance, apart from a light-coloured exterior finish, Tannoy's lower priced MX speaker range (a pair costs about £100) looked much like anybody else's. Meanwhile, the company's top of the range Prestige collection – priced at a wallet-boggling £30,000–£40,000 – still looked much as you imagine speakers must have done back in Tannoy's mid-20th century heyday.

Factory began working for Tannoy in 1998 but, according to Factory director Gavin Thomson, the arrival of Dutch managing director Henny Groenendijk in

Making and buying speakers has always been a bit trainspotterish. The attitude has always been: if it looks good, it must sound terrible.

Stan Vincent, Editor *Hi-Fi Choice* source quoted in *Design*, winter 1996

Founded in 1997, Factory is a London-based consultancy with four creative directors, one business director, four designers and a turnover of £650,000 per year.

Consciously specialising in three-dimensional design, the company claims particular expertise in product design, transport, design strategy, futures, new product development and packaging. Factory routinely collaborates with specialists in market research, graphic design, new media, ergonomics, engineering, interior design, modelmaking and production.

Factory's experience ranges from motorcycles, scooters, aircraft interiors and caravans to telephones, watches, domestic appliances, pens, lighters, trophies, lighting, furniture, packaging and sports equipment. Its clients include British Airways, London Transport, Light Projects, Montblanc, Motorola and Ronson.

Tannoy's New Dimension range marks a modern and lush departure from the visual blandness of its previous products. It features a cherry-wood case trimmed with polished aluminium and velvet.

Opposite and left Factory set out to present the New Dimension range as a finely crafted collection of furniture. The connector block at the back of all future Tannoy speakers will take the distinctive and memorable form of a five-pointed star. 'I think there are a lot of things that you don't notice at first but which make a real difference,' says designer Gavin Thomson.

1999 to work alongside Technical Director Alex Garner gave a new momentum to the company's design policies. 'Henny recognised that while Tannoy's products were still selling and their acoustic technology was highly regarded they had lost their way as a brand,' says Thomson. 'Competitors like Rogers and B&W have been selling on design rather than cost for some years. To compete, Tannoy had to make more of its name and modernise and upgrade the image of its products.' Even so Factory had a delicate path to tread if it was to win over a client and consumers who are both instinctively conservative.

Launched in the autumn of 2000, the New Dimension range provides a first opportunity to assess if the modernisation process has struck the right note. With five speakers of varying sizes priced from £2,000 to £6,000, New Dimension represents the mid-market core of Tannoy's products. The trapezoid form was actually dictated by issues of sound rather than style but the presentation – a cherrywood case trimmed with polished aluminium and black velvet – marks a modern and lush departure from the previous old-fashioned blandness.

Gavin Thomson finds particular satisfaction in the details. 'I think there are a lot of things that you don't notice at first but which make a real difference,' he says. 'For example, we've rationalised the form of the connector block at the back of the speaker into a five-pointed star form which works really well as a cable management system. It's a subtle thing, of course, but I'm hoping that touches like that will become synonymous with Tannoy's design style.'

It is too early to judge if the new range is a success yet but Factory hopes its launch marks the start of a long relationship. 'Sound is sacred to a company like Tannoy and to the people who buy their products. We have tons of ideas for other ranges but educating a company and its customers about what design can achieve takes time,' says Gavin Thomson. 'We are happy to play the long game.'

tko20

Great white hope

The 1990s saw British inventors rethink previously unconsidered domestic objects such as the radiator and the vacuum cleaner from first principles. Now it's the turn of the washing machine.

Britain's inventiveness has often been undermined by the inability of its manufacturers to turn a good idea into a good business* but in the past ten years the emergence of a new generation of innovative British entrepreneurs has provided renewed cause for optimism. The London-based consultancy TKO seems an unlikely candidate to play much of a part in this manufacturing renaissance, however. Since it was founded ten years ago, TKO has consciously targeted Tokyo as the epicentre of its operations, working for a string of Japanese companies including Honda, Sanyo and NEC.

In recent years, however, the company has developed a British string to its bow, playing an important part in the emergence

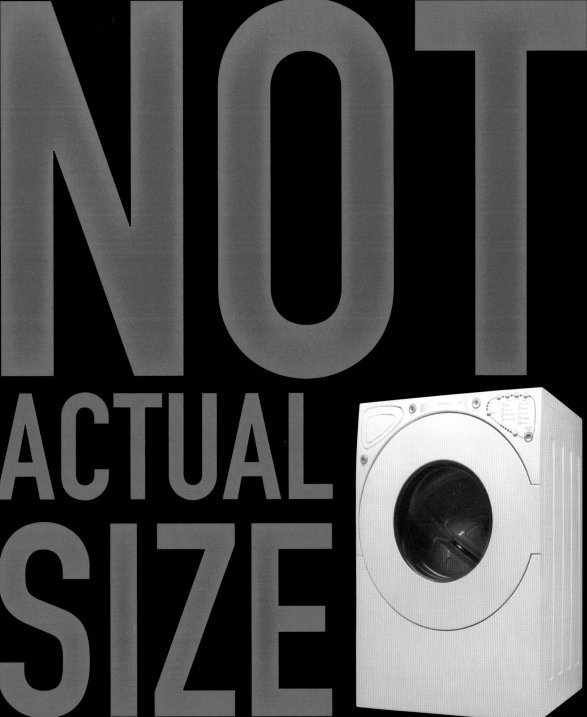

Above in TKO's studio in
London's Covent Garden
prototypes for the Titan
share shelf space with the
company's work for its mainly
Japanese client base.
Right the washing machine
features a drum which can
be removed and used as a
coloured washing basket.

of two of the UK's most promising
manufacturing entrepreneurs. First, in the
mid-1990s, TKO designed the Baygen
clockwork radio that was conceived by
British inventor Trevor Baylis. Since 1996,
the consultancy has been developing and
refining Monotub Industries' Titan washing
machine, scheduled for launch in spring
2001.

The Titan claims to fundamentally rethink
washing machine technology. The large
interior accommodates 40 per cent more
washing than a conventional machine and
there are other benefits: the angle of the
drum – inclined rather than horizontal –
allows easy access to laundry during
loading and unloading and means the
machine can be opened during the cycle
without danger of flooding. Meanwhile the
drum itself removes to double as a brightly-
coloured plastic washing basket.

The Titan is the brainchild of the naval
architect turned accountant and biotech
entrepreneur Martin Myerscough, who
admits to having drawn some inspiration
from the success of the Dyson vacuum
cleaner. Dyson also provided ammunition in

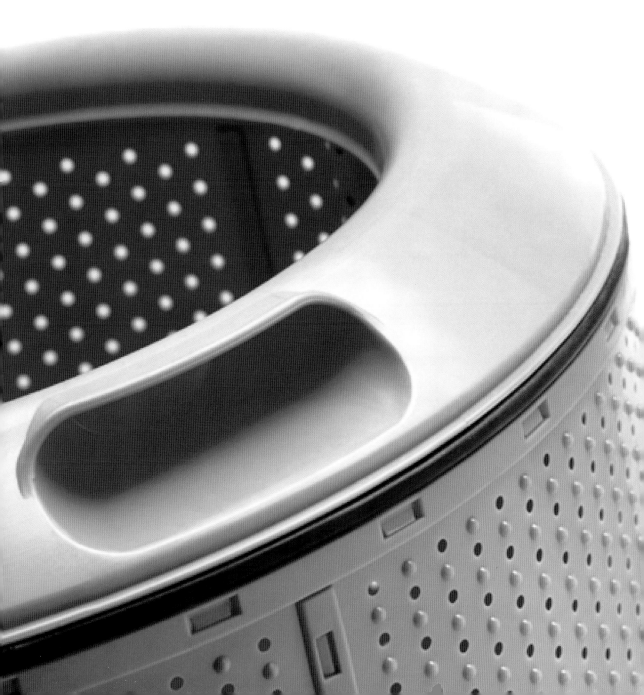

It isn't about novelty. The Titan has to be familiar enough to be recognised as a washing machine.

Anne Gardener partner, TKO

TKO has worked for clients in consumer electronics, telecoms, lighting, housewares, furniture and toys since it was founded by partners Andy Davey and Anne Gardener in January 1990. Davey trained as a product designer but the company no longer sees itself as a product specialist. The company's work now includes software design and qualitative forecasting, and recent projects have included corporate identity and packaging design as well as styling and new product development. In 1996, Andy Davey was awarded the title of BBC Designer of the Year for his work on the Baygen clockwork radio but the consultancy continues to build on its established reputation and track record in Japan, winning two Japanese G-mark good design awards in the last two years. In 2001, TKO will be working on 50/50, a design festival that brings together creative designers and manufacturers from Japan and the UK to work on collaborative projects and products.

Opposite the Titan's understated design consciously follows the established aesthetic and colours of an ordinary washing machine. 'It was vital that we communicated its benefits in a form which still felt comfortable to ordinary users and fitted the dimensions of an ordinary kitchen,' says Anne Gardener.

Monotub Industries' successful campaign to raise an additional £3.5 million worth of investment through the London Alternative Investment Market.

You might have thought that TKO would have chosen to signal the Titan's difference from the competition with eyecatching styling. But apart from providing an extra-large porthole door, TKO decided to take a subtle line. 'It isn't about novelty,' reasons TKO partner Anne Gardener, who led the TKO team. 'The Titan has to be familiar enough to be recognised as a washing machine. It was vital that we communicated its benefits in a form which still felt comfortable to ordinary users and fitted the dimensions of an ordinary kitchen.'

It's taken five years to evolve the Titan into its sleek final form, during which time TKO has worked alongside design engineers Cock and Hen, the in-house team at Monotub and Myerscough himself, honing the original Heath Robinsonian gizmo through 15 prototypes and four separate market research surveys into its final form. But TKO's input into the Titan's design went deeper than its function and appearance. The designers researched and conceived the name of the machine, and designed the corporate identity for Monotub Industries. While the product design process was reaching its conclusion, TKO also designed both product packaging and the Titan website.

In the view of TKO principal Andy Davey the Titan's development story illustrates how British product design skills have grown in the past decade or so. 'Much of the work we do is about keeping our receptors open – predicting and anticipating what is going to happen in a particular marketplace rather than styling an object,' Davey explains. 'Positioning the Titan – an unknown machine made by an unknown company – was a subtle business. We had to look at the product and the brand from a consumer's viewpoint and to consider all the "softer" cultural elements. There is far more to product design today than creating the hardware.'
* The Japanese governmental organisation MITI estimated in 1996 that Britain lost £165 billion from its GNP by failing to take advantage of its own inventions.

priestman goode

Virgin rebirth

Poor timekeeping has threatened to make its West Coast rail franchise an embarrassment to Virgin. But a new train design may yet put the company's image back on track.

There is much work left to do if the growing collection of regional rail franchises is ever to knit together into a seamless and efficient UK national transport network. But there is reason to hope that the privatisation of Britain's railways may yet bring a new and better designed British train in its slipstream. Priestman Goode, the design company currently working on the £1.85 billion five-year contract to redesign and replace Virgin West Coast's entire fleet of engines and rolling stock argues that the rail industry's new market focus is taking UK train design to places it hasn't previously visited. 'Transportation designers usually work for train manufacturers rather than the operators so before privatisation the industry was driven by engineers' priorities rather than those of passengers,' claims Ian

We wanted it to be a British train, but not in the fuddy-duddy way it was something like that and it was meant to be smooth and flowing, but classic and British as well.

Priestman Goode was formed in 1988 and is a partnership between Paul Priestman and Nigel Goode. Today, the company has 17 staff and counts Hitachi, Land Rover and Airbus among its clients. In the past, Priestman Goode's speculative ideas have included a desktop Soft Fan (with 'sails' of silk instead of metal), three deluxe radiators produced by the British company Bisque and a device that babysits the Tamagotchi 'virtual pet'. Priestman Goode now makes products on its own account. In 1997 the company founded Plant, a subsidiary whose output includes Centre Fold, a simple magazine storage system, and the Baby Roll, a mobile nappy changing kit which is sold by Mothercare. Priestman Goode has just designed the First Class environment for the Airbus A3XX and is working on other transportation projects.

* Railtrack is investing £2 billion in the West Coast line's track and signals, which is Europe's biggest rail engineering project. But Britain's rail regulator has expressed doubts that this infrastructure will be completed in time to meet Virgin's timetable.

Priestman Goode drew every single element on the train that the passenger came into contact with: door handles, luggage stacks, seats, coffee points and coat hooks, as well as styling the cab and exterior of the train. It took the design company three months to draw up the designs.

Scoley, the director responsible for Priestman Goode's transport projects. 'But Virgin insisted on having much more say in what their train looked like.'

When Virgin asked Priestman Goode to design a new high-speed tilting train in March 1998 the company specified a vehicle in line with their own faintly offbeat image. 'They wanted the train design to reflect Virgin's qualities: championing customer service and presentation that is fun, surprising and characterful and a bit off the wall,' recalls Scoley. If this sounded like unfamiliar territory to the train manufacturers, they were in good company. 'Our only transport project on the books at that point was the Virgin Atlantic seat but Virgin thought our inexperience would make for concepts that were fresh,' says Scoley. 'And the urgent time frame meant it was very spontaneous.'

'Urgent' is understating it a bit. Priestman Goode designed and built the first prototype nose section in a mere four weeks. Sleek and streamlined with a silver, red and yellow livery resembling a stretched bullseye, the prototype effectively established the character of the train which they viewed as 'the natural successor to the British Rail 125'. 'We wanted it to be a bit of an icon but not in the fashionable way something like the Ford Ka is,' says Scoley. 'It's meant to be smooth and fluid but classic and British as well.'

When the early concept received the go-ahead, Priestman Goode set about applying the design in detail. The company's first task was to work alongside interiors and graphics specialists in drawing up a coherent Virgin 'red book' that laid down every element of the design to the manufacturers. 'We drew every single element on the train that the passenger came into contact with: door handles, luggage stacks, coffee points, even the coat hooks,' recalls Ian Scoley. 'It took three months.'

Demanding as this process was, the real challenge was ensuring that the design wasn't compromised in the making. 'Every element – doors, windows, kitchens, seats – seemed to be made by a separate company but few of them had ever had much dealings with designers,' says Scoley. 'It was a struggle and we often had to take a softly-softly approach to get our way, but the key ultimately was that we had Virgin's trust and its authority behind us and they haven't wilted under pressure.'

Customers are now able to judge for themselves as the first complete prototype for the train has now been launched. It remains to be seen if Railtrack will be able to deliver their part of the bargain* but if all goes well the train will go into service early in 2002 and Virgin claims that by 2005 the average rail journey from Manchester to London will be cut to two hours.

By then, Priestman Goode hope they will be viewed not just as product designers but as transport and environmental specialists too. The company has already received an enquiry from a manufacturer of ocean liners. 'Product design is too limited as a definition of what we do,' explains Ian Scoley. 'And while it's demanding to work with companies that are going through big cultural changes, transport offers the sort of diversity product designers dream of.'

seymour powell**33**

Leather engineering

The buoyant market for luxury goods may find industrial designers encroaching on territory traditionally occupied by craftspeople or fashion designers.

Since it was founded in 1984 Seymour Powell has designed products including cordless kettles and steam irons for Tefal, motorbikes for Norton and MZ and watches for Baby G. In recent years, the practice founders Richard Seymour and Dick Powell have emerged as TV personalities in the UK, thanks to their appearances on the Channel Four programmes *Designs on Your...* and *Better by Design* in which they have created new concepts for, among other things, the toilet, the kitchen bin, the shopping trolley, the lifejacket and the razor. One of the concepts for their first series, a bra for British manufacturer Charnos, went into production in October 2000.

Connolly wanted something masculine and pure that made the most of their British automotive heritage and which was a step up from the Cartier or Vuitton equivalent.

Opposite and above each item in the Connolly range was intended to have a distinguishing feature of its own, but details such as the locks concealed beneath leather flaps also provide a consistent family language.

Seymour Powell is already one of Britain's better-known design consultancies but while its mass-market product portfolio extends from watches and cameras to steam irons and even bras, it is not the sort of company you readily associate with a highly crafted range of handmade calf-skin luggage. 'We would have been unlikely to get this sort of commission ten or even five years ago,' admits Seymour Powell associate director Nick Talbot. Talbot believes Connolly Luxury Goods was attracted by Seymour Powell's experience in designing motorbikes and cars. 'But I think they also wanted designers who knew how to design products with a sense of individuality that were practical and not too expensive to make,' ventures Talbot.

Connolly Luxury Goods had originally been a subsidiary of Connolly Brothers, a 'tanner of hides' previously best known for providing manufacturers such as Ferrari and Aston Martin with their immaculate and fragrant leather car interiors. Connolly Luxury Goods represented the company's bid to broaden its appeal. The idea was to produce a range of clothes, bags, gloves and other leather goods which made the most of the Connolly name and heritage.

Seymour Powell's involvement in the project began in June 1997 shortly after the brand was bought by Isabel Ettedgui, the wife of Joseph, owner of the eponymous chain of upmarket fashion shops. Isabel's plan to relaunch Connolly Luxury Goods involved expanding the collection and selling it through a new store in London's West End. A distinctive new luggage range was a particular priority. Connolly wanted something masculine and pure that made the most of its British automotive heritage and which was a step up from the Cartier or Vuitton equivalent. 'In some senses, I found it a bit like working on a vehicle,' says Nick Talbot. 'You need to reduce the amount of material used, to keep the number of components to a minimum and to minimise weight – leather is very heavy.'

In one important way, however, the project was unlike anything the designers had faced with their mass-manufacturing clients. 'We are used to thinking about making things in their thousands and

Left and below Seymour Powell's studio is in a converted chapel in west London. **Opposite** Seymour Powell found working with crafted leather a more artisanal process than handling their usual mass production materials such as plastic and metal.

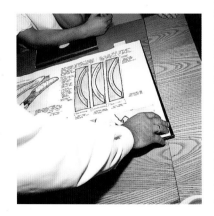

pushing the potential of industrial materials like plastic and metal to the limit,' says Nick Talbot. 'But if you want to make the most of leather, you can't just produce drawings. You have to tap into the knowledge of expert craftsmen and get them to test out your ideas by producing and refining a series of prototypes.'

The result of this six month process of 'leather engineering' was an ultra-simple looking seven-piece set. Each piece features an exterior panel trimmed with an edge of etched aluminium, concealing behind it the lock which is recessed into the surface of the bag. The idea is both to allow owners more privacy when they are opening their case and to provide a subtle and intriguing sense of visual unity, but Seymour Powell insists that the 'family' feel does not detract from the distinctiveness of products. 'It was important that products that were quite expensive – they cost from £200 to £2,000 – each had its own particular bit of magic,' says Nick Talbot. 'For example the handles all look similar but the attaché case mechanism has a hidden extension which allows you turn it into a

shoulder bag and gives a satisfying "pop" whenever you use it.'

Since its launch in autumn 2000, 'Aeromotive', as the range is called, has done well, with the attaché case proving almost as popular with women as with men. Seymour Powell is keen to do more work in a similar mould. 'There's enormous potential for fine hand-made things but craft is shaking off its old-fashioned image and its worthy overtones,' argues Nick Talbot. 'The interesting thing about this range is that it would fit as comfortably into the cockpit of a Gulf-stream jet as it would in the boot of an Aston Martin.'

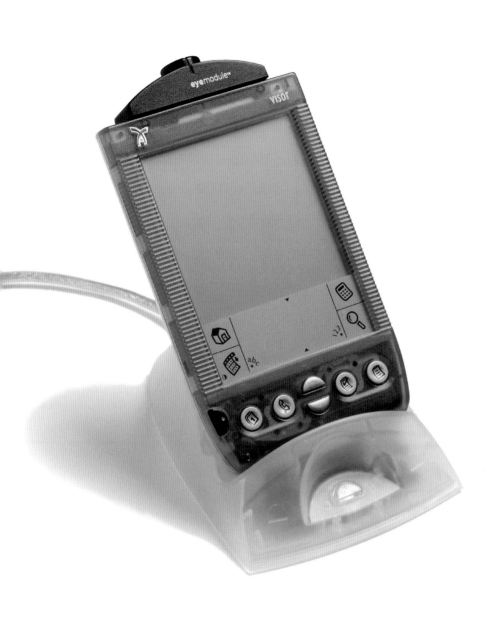

ideo39

California teaming

Product designers have always dreamt of 'cutting out the middleman' by creating their own products. Now a new generation of digital products may finally break the manufacturing mould.

In the 20 years since it was founded, IDEO has evolved into one of the few global companies specialising in new product development. The company currently maintains offices in California, London, Tokyo and seven other sites worldwide. IDEO claims to offer 'complete innovation and design services from strategy and concept development to engineering and production' and counts specialists from fields including human factors, cognitive psychology and business strategy as well as industrial designers, engineers, architects and software specialists among its 350 employees. Clients for its products, services and environments range from the BBC to BMW and Nike to Nokia.

We like to think about new ways of doing business. Developing our own products provides our people with new creative and commercial incentives.

Ingelise Nielsen head of marketing, IDEO

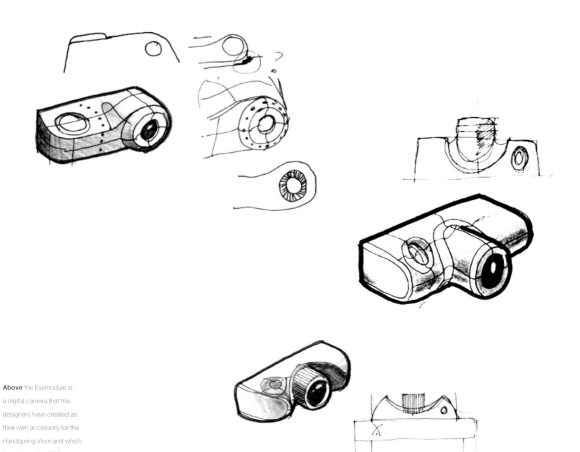

Above the Eyemodule is a digital camera that the designers have created as their own accessory for the Handspring Visor and which is produced by IDEO's own manufacturing subsidiary.

If the Eyemodule camera turns out to be a success, its example could provide an intriguing blueprint for the way technologically driven products are created in the 21st century. The Eyemodule is an accessory designed by IDEO for the Handspring Visor hand-held computer and owes its genesis to a distinctly Californian model of digital entrepreneurship.

The Visor project emerged from IDEO's long-term relationship with Californian digital technology pioneer Donna Dubinski, onetime co-founder of Palm and now the owner of hand-held computer manufacturer Handspring. Though born in the UK, the biggest of IDEO's ten worldwide offices is now in Silicon Valley and the design consultancy had already successfully collaborated with Dubinski on the creation of the Palm V.* When they developed the Handspring Visor, the first product in a new family of handheld computers based on the 3Com Palm operating system, it was natural that Handspring should turn to IDEO.

The essence of the Handspring Visor's appeal is the expandability that it brings to the Personal Digital Assistant. It features an 'expansion slot' that accepts a variety of plug-in modules so the computer can interface with accessories such as wireless modems, pagers, MP3 players and games, as well as providing standard calendar, contact and notepad functions. IDEO's industrial designers and electrical and mechanical engineers spent a year honing both the form and the mechanical design of the Visor ** but they also began to realise that the project potentially offered IDEO more than a design role. 'The principle behind the Handspring is that the Springboard expansion slot provides opportunities for companies to partner with Handspring and add modular applications. In that sense it is a bit like a grown up Gameboy,' explains Ingelise Nielsen, IDEO's head of marketing. 'Since we knew the technology and the device so well it seemed the perfect opportunity to develop a module of our own.'

IDEO brainstorms and a fast track development process produced the Eyemodule, a tiny digital camera designed specifically for the Handspring's expansion slot which captures images in colour or

Above and left IDEO's London office includes modelmaking facilities. **Below** IDEO worked 'hand in glove' with Donna Dubinski on the creation of both the Palm V and the Handspring Visor so the company was well equipped to develop its own Handspring accessory.

Opposite the sort of collaborative partnership between manufacturers and designers that led to the creation of the Eyemodule is increasingly common in Silicon Valley and may represent a powerful precedent for techno-driven 21st-century manufacturing culture.

prototyping
in progress

black and white. Images are viewed in real time on the Visor's screen and captured using a single or multiple image timer. These images can be beamed to other Palm OS devices or be saved and printed or emailed from a Windows PC. The product is being manufactured by Blocks Products, the manufacturing arm of IDEO.

In product design, the spirit of manufacturing enterprise that underpins a concept like Handspring remains largely a Silicon Valley phenomenon as yet but Ingelise Nielsen believes that 'as the New Economy takes off, it's beginning to happen on this side of the Atlantic too.'

IDEO has started an initiative in the area of venture funding to explore how to integrate a more entrepreneurial strain to the company's business strategy. Now IDEO is already working with – and/or investing in – several new media start-ups in Europe and the US and integrating these ventures, along with the Handspring Visor, into its existing profit share scheme. 'We're very cautious about the ideas we are prepared to invest in,' says Ingelise Nielsen. 'But we like to think about new ways of doing

business. Developing our own products provides our people with new creative and commercial incentives. It's not going to become the core of our business but it does reflect on our creativity as consultants. It must give clients an extra sense of confidence if their designers are ready and willing to invest in their ideas.'

* Palm computers were a runaway success, catapulting the company into the lead in the handheld PC market with around 70–80% market share, strides ahead of its nearest competitor, Microsoft PocketPC. Source: *The Guardian*, 4 September 2000
** Market newcomer Handspring has proved a point or two with its low-priced Visor, which cleverly targeted the youth market and won, and now commands roughly a quarter of the US PDA market. Source: *The Guardian*, 4 September 2000

Switzerland calling

Communications technology has become a 21st-century boom zone. No wonder Swatch was keen to bring some of its brand values to the telephone.

Since its formation in 1988, PSD Associates, based in Richmond, Surrey, has created an unusual mix of design competencies which aim to help companies develop new brands and services. PSD emphasises an integrated approach to product design, 2D/3D packaging, brand development, digital media and graphic communication. Its client list includes Adshel, BT, Virgin, Mitsubishi and Philips and projects include the packaging for Van den Bergh Foods' Chicken Tonight Sizzle and Stir sauces, a new corporate identity for Swiss crayon manufacturers Caran d'Ache, an award-winning website for Flymo, the powered garden equipment manufacturer, and Virgin Airline's drive-through check-in facility for first-class passengers.

* Intel is now reckoned to be the world's 7th most valuable brand with a value of $30 billion. The Finnish mobile phone company Nokia is the world's most valuable non-US brand with an estimated value of $21 billion, while Swedish competitor Ericsson is 17th with a brand value of $15 billion. Coca-Cola continues to lead the market with an estimated value of $84 billion, ahead of Microsoft ($57 billion) and IBM ($44 billion). Source: Interbrand/Citibank, 1999

Technological boom over the past decade has brought recognition and prosperity to a new generation of innovation-conscious manufacturers, among them computer specialists like Intel and mobile phone giants like Nokia and Ericsson.* And the new competitive and innovative climate is inevitably encouraging more established businesses and brands to rethink their product strategies for the 21st century.

Swatch is best known for its achievement in creating a highly successful global brand in the 1980s by reinventing the watch as a cheap and collectable fashion item. But as the millennium approached, the Swiss company also began turning its attention to technological convergence. In the early 1990s, Swatch made the decision to move into the telecommunications market by developing and making a range of Swatch-branded cordless telephones.

The West London-based design consultancy PSD, a telecoms veteran thanks to its experience in working for Motorola, was the company chosen to design a range of phones and packaging with a common visual personality which chimed with Swatch's established 'personality'. It was, as PSD director Steve Hughes recalls, an exciting if daunting challenge. 'Swatch is a demanding company to design for because almost everyone has a very clear idea in his or her own mind what one of their products should look and feel like,' says Hughes. 'In one sense that's a great help when you're designing something but it also puts tremendous pressure on a designer. If the product doesn't feel "Swatchy", customers will spot it immediately.'

The result of a 12-month design and development programme, the Dect 1 set out to translate 'Swatchiness' – which had been identified by the manufacturer as 'joy of life', 'positive provocation', 'imaginative & trend-setting', 'good value' and 'high quality' – into a cordless digital phone that looked as visually innovative and seductive as the company's range of watches. Launched in 1995, the phone's translucent and curvaceous, candy-coloured plastic tones were intended as a characteristically vibrant Swatch response to the monochrome homogeneity of domestic telephones. The

Opposite PSD's studio in Richmond, West London. The company is unusual in having used its expertise in product design as the basis for expansion as a broad-based multidisciplinary design consultancy.

Everyone has a very clear idea in his or her own mind of what a Swatch product should be like… If the product doesn't feel 'Swatchy', customers will spot it immediately.

Steve Hughes director, PSD

upright-mounted form – combining a charger, phone and answer machine – was quickly nicknamed 'the lighthouse' by the company and literally aimed to make the telephone stand out.

PSD was also conscious that for a product which sold for a pricey £300 per unit to attract sufficient customers it needed to be functionally as well as aesthetically innovative. 'The beauty of the design was that you could take the charger off the main unit and use it separately so that you could operate six handsets from one base station,' explains Steve Hughes. 'It was a feature calculated to appeal to the sort of small, design-conscious businesses that we thought might be the early adopters of a Swatch phone.'

Dect 1 proved an immediate success in continental Europe, particularly in the Italian and German markets. Within a month, Swatch had sold three times as many phones as expected. The past five years have seen PSD continue to hone the concept. In 1998 a second Swatch cordless phone was launched, this one featuring an answerphone integrated into the handset. Dect 3, which launched in 2001, takes the evolution a stage further. The product features a mounting device which gives the impression that the handset is floating unsupported above its charger base.

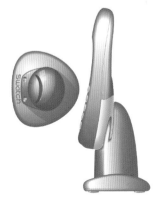

Opposite, left and below
the latest version of the
Swatch cordless phone
features a mounting device
adapted from a menu holder
which gives the impression
that the handset is floating
unsupported on its charger.

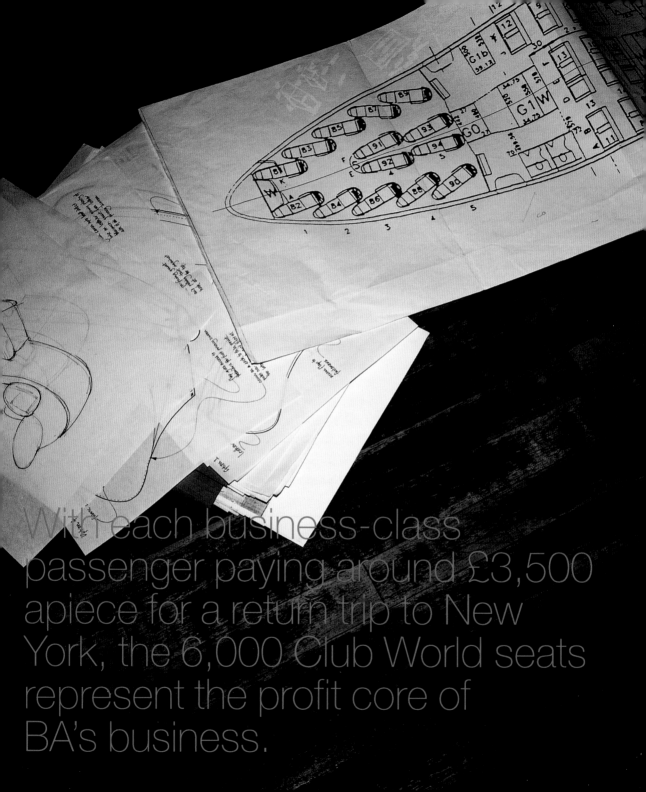

With each business-class passenger paying around £3,500 apiece for a return trip to New York, the 6,000 Club World seats represent the profit core of BA's business.

tangerine51

Flying flat out

Every airline is intent on proclaiming the virtues of its business-class seat. Now British Airways claims to have created the first flat bed in the sky.

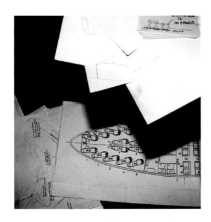

* Club World passengers account for approximately £1.65 billion of BA's business, economy passengers a mere £700 million. Source: BA figures

Below left the new seat features a fully reclining chair with three different sitting positions and an adjustable footstool that combine to convert into a flat bed. Opposite a model of the design in Tangerine's south east London studio

Vague promises about the comfort and luxury of first and business-class facilities have always featured large in airline TV advertising. But now the desire to gain an edge, particularly on competitive transatlantic routes, is encouraging airlines to pay serious attention to the challenge of creating a truly comfortable 'chair in the air'. The past five years have seen international carriers from Cathay Pacific to Virgin Atlantic reshaping their first and business-class seats and most of the American companies have come up with new chairs too.

British Airways has been in the thick of the battle since 1996 when the company introduced a 'bed in the sky', designed by consultants Design Acumen, in its first-class cabin. Despite reducing capacity from 18 to 14, the concept was a great success, almost doubling sales. The business-class seat represented an even bigger challenge for the 25 or so design consultancies that were asked to pitch for the project. More than 100 BA 747s and 777s ply the transatlantic routes and with each business-class passenger paying around £3,500 apiece for a return trip to

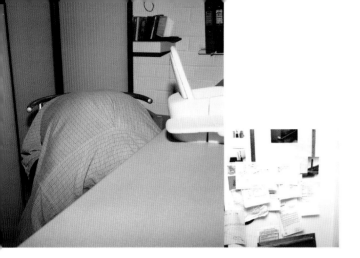

New York, the 6,000 or so Club World seats represent the profit core of the company's business.*

Naturally then, Martin Darbyshire of Tangerine was delighted when his company won a five-way competitive pitch to design a seat which specified 'privacy, flexibility and a good night's sleep' as key. But he admits he was a little daunted too. 'You have to realise that the constraints in a cabin redesign are enormous. Fuel represents 30 per cent of overheads so you can't really increase weight too much,' claims Darbyshire. 'That's why, while there are exceptions, like Virgin Atlantic's new seat, 80 per cent of the changes we have seen so far in airline seats have been cosmetic in all but name.'

The complexities of creating a chair that balanced these cost and comfort considerations and met aviation's strict safety regulations can be gauged by its cost (£200 million) and the length of the design development process. It took a mere three weeks for Tangerine to come up with a concept but then a further three months to build a full-size model, three

more to refine the chair and finally six months' work for four staff working 13 hours a day with seat manufacturer Britax to turn the Club World seat into a reality.

A study of the finished product reveals that there is nothing cosmetic about Tangerine's redesign. The new seat features a fully reclining chair with three different sitting positions and an adjustable footstool that combine to convert into a flat bed. 'The idea is that the footstool mimics the elements that give comfort in the home,' says Martin Darbyshire. 'And we've tried to extend that concept to the in-flight entertainment system. You can watch comfortably whatever position the seat is in.'

Given the complexity of the redesign it was inevitable that the whole of the Club World cabin would have to be reconfigured to accommodate the concept. Seats are now grouped in pairs with half of passengers now sitting with their backs to the pilot. 'We asked 2,500 people if they would mind flying backwards,' says Darbyshire. 'In fact, the research concluded that the new configuration was less

regimented and more human.'

It remains to be seen if the advantages of a product that was first introduced in March 2000 will make up for the reduction in seats. But Martin Darbyshire believes that the new sense of comfort will provide a winning sales incentive. 'This is the first seat to treat passengers as if they were at home rather than the dentist,' he says. 'I think it will prove you can put a price on a good night's sleep.'

Tangerine was founded in 1989 by Clive Grinyer, Martin Darbyshire, Peter Phillips and Jonathan Ive (who went on to find fame as designer of the Apple iMac). Its ten full and part-time staff generate an annual turnover of around £1 million.

Tangerine's client list features companies from the USA, Japan and Korea as well as Britain and mainland Europe. Among them are Ideal Standard, Wedgwood Waterford, LG Electronics, Samsung, Hitachi and Unilever.

The whole of the Club World cabin had to be reconfigured to accommodate the concept with half of the passengers now sitting backwards. Fortunately, with the three-dimensional sophistication of computer-generated design (CAD), designers and managers were able to 'walk around and sit in' the new seat long before it was built.

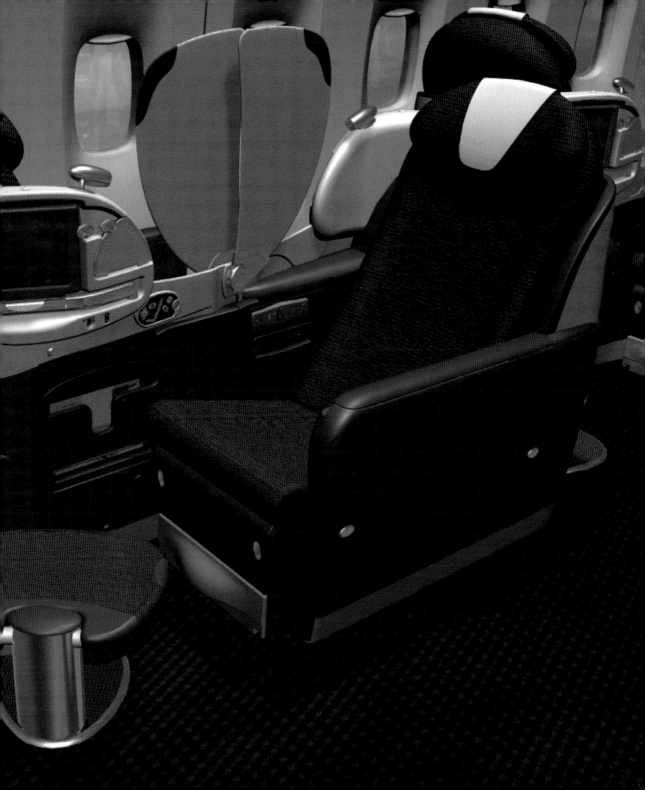

Case history

Manufacturers expect instant results from designers but the enduring relationship between Samsonite and FM Design shows the benefits of a long-term design strategy.

'There are two kinds of industrial design clients,' says Richard Miles, partner at FM Design: 'the choppers and changers who want immediate results and those prepared to invest in a long-term relationship.' There's not much doubt which category Samsonite falls into. The American company has been making luggage in Europe for 35 years or so and for the past 20 has been an FM client. 'At first, their desire was simply to adapt their existing US range to the European market, but American companies often seem immensely innovation conscious,'* says Miles. 'Samsonite has changed enormously since we started working with it.' As the company's product range has expanded, so too have its manufacturing capabilities. Samsonite now has factories in India, South

America and China in addition to the existing facilities in Europe and the US. Its ambitions now transcend luggage too: Samsonite has even launched a Prada-influenced diffusion range of shoes and clothes sold through its own shops in London, Milan, Brussels and other European cities.

FM's contribution to this pattern of global growth started in earnest with the design and development of the Oyster range of plastic suitcases of which 18.5 million have been sold since the Mark One version first appeared in 1986. There are several companies like Samsonite now using injection-moulded polypropylene as a material for making luggage, and the Oyster design – in particular the ultra-secure three-latch form which eliminated the need for a

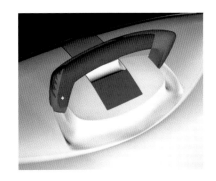

It's not like designing a mobile phone which is out of date in a few months. These designs are expected to last at least ten years.

Richard Miles partner, FM Design

* The USA is the world's most innovative country according to the views of Britain's top businessmen. When asked to name the three countries they considered most innovative, 95 per cent named the USA, 66 per cent named Britain and 40 per cent, Japan. Source: MORI/3M Captains of Industry survey 1999

** The advantage of these over cases with traditional corner wheels is that all the weight stays on the ground; the retractable handles can be adjusted to your height, so there's no need for stooping.

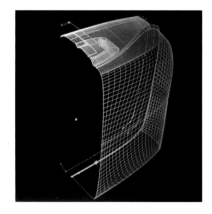

Opposite and above like all product designers FM does much of its design work on computer, but the company's Islington studio also features a workshop in which prototypes can be hand turned.

costly and heavy metal frame – has set a benchmark for rivals such as Delsey and Carlton to match. 'It's quite consciously intended to be the ideal suitcase for the age of air travel,' says Miles. 'Light and robust enough to last almost indefinitely.'

Designing a suitcase is a more difficult creative challenge than it might appear. 'It's a complete design job, not just a bit of styling,' argues Miles. 'It's a product which has to work as well on the inside as it does outside.' Since the launch of the original Oyster, FM has designed a series of new luggage ranges including System 4 (a luxury range made of ABS plastic) Epsilon (a 'high-end' polypropylene range) and Magnum (a low-cost self-assembly case).

Perhaps the most demanding challenge for FM has been launching a successor to Samsonite's flagship Oyster range. 'It takes a lot of thinking about,' says Miles 'because you don't want to throw out the baby with the bath water.' Technically, FM opted for evolution rather than revolution. The second Oyster retains the fundamentals of the originals such as the three-latch form but the Mark Two suitcase range is lighter and a

new pair of upright suitcases** has been added, along with better wheel systems across the range.

But the biggest difference between the two ranges is their styling. Just as a 1980s BMW would seem rectilinear and angular in comparison to its 1990s equivalent, so the 1998 Oyster is soft and organic in contrast to the crisp and sharp form of its 1980s incarnation. The automotive metaphor is a useful one since investments required in tooling and production make longevity a key issue for Samsonite. 'It is like gearing up to produce a car,' says Miles. 'It's not like designing a mobile phone which is out of date in a few months. These designs are expected to last at least ten years.'

The success of the strategy can be gauged by the Oyster's sales figures. Whereas the launch of a new model BMW usually means the end of its predecessor, Oyster Mark One appears to have achieved classic status. 'It was intended as a replacement but they're selling side by side,' says Richard Miles. 'It's the greatest feeling if you're a designer when customers vote with their feet.'

FM Design was formed in 1988 by Ben
Fether and Richard Miles whose design
partnership dates back a further ten years.
FM's design projects over that time have
included packaging for Procter & Gamble,
toys for Hasbro, office systems for
Steelcase, cinema seating for Virgin and
train interiors for SNCF. One of its padlocks
for Yale is in the permanent collection of the
Museum of Modern Art in New York. Today
the FM team consists of 25 designers,
modelmakers and support staff. Among
its latest projects is a comprehensive range
of office furniture and accessories for
Gunlocke, an American company which
focuses on the 'professional and executive
market'.

Opposite and below

the greatest difference
between the two Oyster
ranges is their styling. While
the 1980s range was crisp
and sharp, the 1998 Oyster is
soft and organic. The second
range was intended to replace
the first but in fact the two
cases continue to sell side
by side.

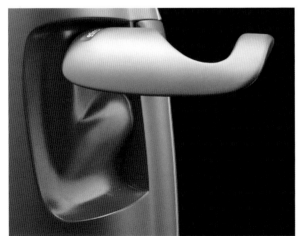

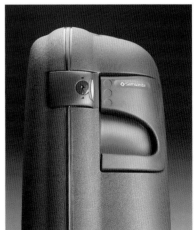

frazer
designers**62**

A remote personality

Sky Broadcasting is among a new wave of global service and technology corporations using product design to reinforce their corporate personalities.

Based in North London, Frazer Designers has been helping clients turn new technology into practical products for well over 20 years. Its products include everything from the early TV games of the 1970s to today's portable communication devices. The company has a particular expertise in the design of electrical and computer-related products for business and consumer markets and boasts a strong engineering team as well as product designers. The company's clients include Acer, Alcatel, NEC, Philips, Securicor, Sky and Vision Engineering.

Below and opposite Frazer
Designers created 30 initial
prototypes for the Sky Remote
handset in its north London
studio.

For the first time, the customer has something tangible which they can think of as a Sky product and which subtly enhances its brand.

Stephen Frazer partner, Frazer Designers

The emergence of an elite group of technology companies as the world's most valuable brands is already a well established millennial trend.* But since much of the output of this corporate new wave consists of software and media services, you might not expect these digital giants to offer new opportunities for product designers.

Curiously, however, Frazer Designers' most widely distributed product at the end of the 20th century was created for one of the most visible of the new media giants. Commissioned in July 1996, the Frazer-designed remote control handset for Sky Broadcasting has become a ubiquitous feature of British living rooms. Since its high-profile launch in October 1998, around five million units have been distributed in the UK. 'It would have been hard to imagine an industrial designer having a client like Sky a few years ago let alone a product like this one,' claims Frazer Designers' founding partner Stephen Frazer.

Frazer explains that the decision to commission the handset was driven by Sky's desire to reinforce its image. 'Its

*Yahoo!, only launched in 1994, is reportedly worth more than General Motors, Texaco and Merrill Lynch, while Amazon.com had a quoted value of $25 billion in March 2000.
Source: *The Future of Brands* (Interbrand Group) quoted in *Design in Britain*, March 2000

According to nearly a third of UK businesses, more than half of business will be done over the Internet by 2002.
Source: Design Council research quoted in *Design in Britain*, 2000

product range costs from £40 or so to around £400 but Sky's customers didn't really have anything that represented the company,' says Frazer. 'It uses the terms of product design but its prime function is to establish Sky as the official gatekeeper of digital TV.'

Not, Frazer insists, that traditional product design values took second place to branding. Briefed to create 'the most comfortable and easy-to-use remote ever for males and females between the ages of 5 and 80', the designers were intent on avoiding the shortcomings of existing design. 'We tried to ignore other handsets and to go back to first principles,' says Frazer partner Jonathan Knight.

An initial series of 30 foam models was whittled down to a short list of six which were tested blindfold both by the client and by independent focus groups. The final design – created after nine months' development and testing and manufactured at a tooling cost alone of £250,000 – is a robust asymmetrical unit shaped like a sycamore seed.

Frazer argues that the flat and balanced

shape and the configuration of the buttons make the Sky product the most ergonomic remote handset ever created, citing the low rate of product returns – only 100 out of five million – as evidence of customer satisfaction. Meanwhile, Sky has adopted the remote control as a marketing symbol which continues to feature large in the company's promotional and advertising programmes. 'For the first time, the customer has something tangible which they can think of as a Sky product and which subtly enhances its brand,' argues Stephen Frazer.

It is a little early to say whether the remote control 'helps shift public perceptions of Sky as a media bully boy to that of a caring supplier', as Frazer hopes it might. What does seem certain, however, is that the Sky remote control handset represents an early example of a new breed of product – part tool, part brand symbol – that will become increasingly common among global corporations as the digital media and communication revolution picks up momentum.

Opposite and right

the remote control handset
has featured large in Sky's
marketing campaigns. Frazer
claims that its asymmetrical,
flat and balanced form makes
it 'the most ergonomic
handset ever made'.

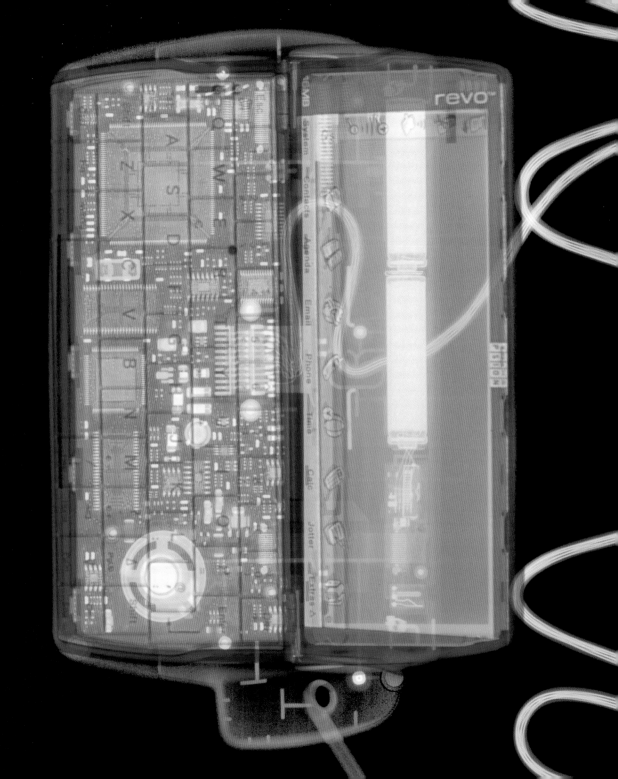

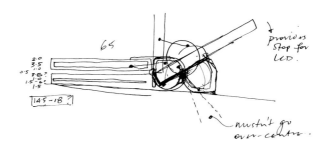

Size matters

A stable relationship with its designers has been fundamental to Psion's success as a manufacturer of hand-held computers. But technological convergence may present the Therefore partnership with its biggest challenge yet.

Therefore was formed in March 1993 and now has 25 industrial designers and engineers working in its London office generating a turnover of around £2 million.

Founded with the backing of Psion, Therefore naturally has considerable experience in the design of technologically driven products such as computers and mobile phones, but the company has continued to expand its range, now claiming expertise in areas such as toys, medical products, hi-fi, aviation and domestic appliances.

The company's clients include Psion, Symbian, Motorola, NEC, GE, Virgin, Avery, Naim and Abbot Labs.

Opposite Therefore has been honing the classic 'clam-shell' form of the Psion for almost a decade. **Above right** recent improvements include a stable hinge which stops the Psion from toppling over when the 'touchscreen' is used.

Opposite and below the
Therefore studio in west
London. The company's
partnership with Psion has
flourished for nearly ten years,
while chief designer Martin
Riddiford has worked for
Psion since 1983.

The key to a good result, designers will tell you, is a good brief. But the truism doesn't appear to apply to the Psion Revo. 'We didn't really need a brief because it seemed such a natural development of the Series 5. Psion wanted new product ideas and so we started working on the concept without being asked,' says Martin Riddiford, the director of the Revo design team at Therefore design consultants. 'Almost as soon as the concept landed on the managing director's desk, he decided to put it into production.'

If the designer seems nonchalant about the creation of the Revo, it isn't altogether surprising. Riddiford is one designer who can justifiably claim to know his client's product inside out. Since he started working with Psion in 1983 (while he was at Frazer Designers), Riddiford has designed all seven of the company's ranges. He has witnessed from close up the British company's first steps as a manufacturer of electronic diaries in the mid-1980s, its successful emergence as a producer of 'personal organisers' in the 1990s and its ascent to global status as a full-blown

manufacturer of handheld computers and a software pioneer that even Bill Gates takes seriously.

There is little doubt that the stability of its relationship with its chief designer has been almost as fundamental to the success of one of Britain's few independent computer hardware manufacturers as the company's much vaunted Symbian software platform. Perhaps the key moment came in 1991 with the launch of the Series 3, the first design combining the Psion's cunning 'double-hinge' opening mechanism and the clam-shell format that made the 'electronic Filofax' a 1990s cult object.

In the years since, Therefore has responded to Psion's continuing leaps in processing power, dividing its design group into two teams, with key designers such as Charlie Colquhoun honing its graphic user interface (GUI) and Steve de Saulles adding new ergonomic touches and improving the presentation of the machine's hardware.

The Series 5 featured a proper keyboard, a stylus interface and a redesigned hinge which ensures that the machine remains stable, however hard you

Above, previous page and

opposite so close is the

relationship between designer

and manufacturer that

Therefore created the design

for the Revo 'on spec'. It is

'aimed at mobile phone users

rather than serious computer

heads,' says Therefore's

Martin Riddiford.

poke at the 'touch' screen. First launched in September 1999, the Revo is its pocket-sized equivalent. 'It's smaller, lighter, cheaper (around £250) and aimed at mobile phone users rather than serious computer heads. You can use it to exchange contacts with infra red connections, send email and so on,' says Martin Riddiford. 'Psion's advertising slogan was "Get organised. Get connected". That summed up its appeal. It's a personal accessory in the same way that a mobile phone is.'

The continuing appeal of the Psion format can be judged by the Revo's sales figures – more than 250,000 have been sold since the product's launch in September 1999 – but Martin Riddiford admits that the greatest challenge is yet to come. 'Convergence between mobiles, laptops and communication networks means there's no room for complacency,' he says.

The emergence of popular American hand-held competitors such as the Handspring and Palm has muddied the waters for 'Personal Digital Assistants' and it remains to be seen what impact the much hyped Bluetooth mobile technology and Ericsson's R380 Symbian-driven Web-enabled phone (launched in September 2000) will have on Psion's marketplace.*
'I don't think we can be certain what form the Psion will take five years from now. Advances in software will drive the shape of the product. It will be up to us to adapt to a technological landscape that is changing before your very eyes.'
* By next year, according to the publicist for Symbian, there will be '30 or so' mobile 'communicators' or 'smartphones' or 'wireless information devices' for sale. Source: *Guardian Online*, October 2000.

In October 1998, Bill Gates himself 'leaked' a Microsoft memo to the US media identifying Psion as his vast corporation's 'Number One Global Threat'.

Guardian Online, February 2000

design council74

The Design Council is the UK's national authority on design. It inspires and enables the use of effective design on a strategic level by UK business in the world context and also works to raise design's profile within the education system.

In addition, its activities include encouraging government to act as an exemplar of the use of design thinking, and it also places great importance on working in partnership with other influential organisations in business, education and government.

Through the Millennium Products initiative, the Design Council has promoted the excellence of British design and innovation both to audiences in the UK and on the world stage. In the closing years of the 1990s, the project identified 1,012 products and services which challenged convention, solved problems, provided benefits to their users, employed technology in innovative ways and opened up new opportunities.

The stories behind these products – how they were inspired and developed and what impact they have had – are now freely available on the Design Council website and are being used as the basis for events, publications, educational materials, tools and other initiatives. New Innovation Stories are continually being gathered to provide more inspiring examples of how business can benefit from good design.

The Design Council has embarked on a growing programme of international activity to promote British design, centred on touring exhibitions featuring Millennium Products and backed by events for business people. These exhibitions have had an enthusiastic welcome in four continents since 1998, and 2001 will see the most ambitious yet, in the shape of a display in New York's Grand Central Station as part of the two-week UKinNY festival.

In the UK, the Design Council's major activities include Design in Business Week and Design in Education Week, both of which are nationwide initiatives. It also communicates its messages through media projects, such as the *Designs on Your…* TV series featuring Richard Seymour and Dick Powell, and devotes resources to research. Both through the annual publication *Design in Britain* and its website, the Design Council provides access to research showing how its audiences view design and innovation and covering other topics including the design industry and the impact of emerging and future trends.

For more information about the Design Council, visit **www.designcouncil.org.uk**

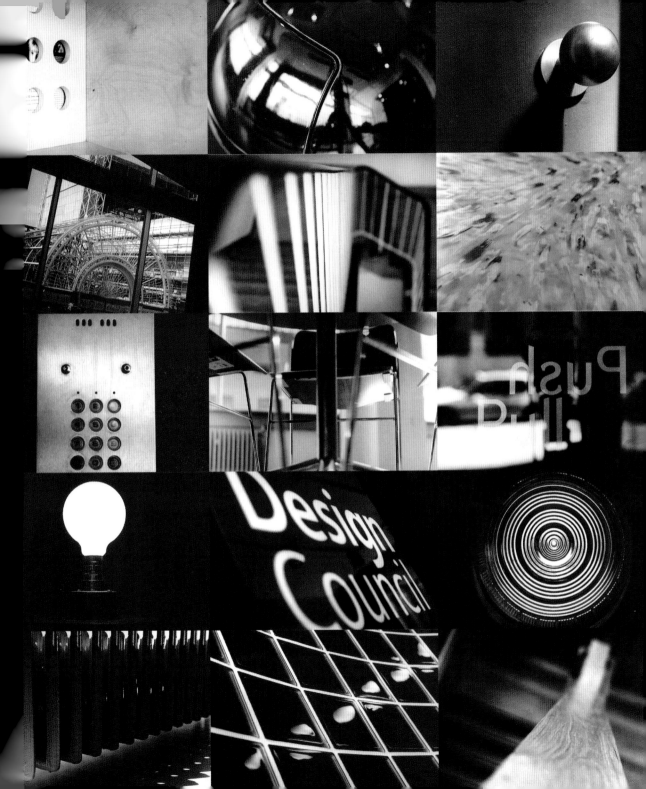

trade partners uk76

Trade Partners UK is the lead Government trade support service for British companies trading in world markets. It brings together teams in more than 200 embassies and posts overseas, more than 45 Business Links in the UK and at least nine Government Departments, as well as representatives in Chambers of Commerce across the country.

The principal role of Trade Partners UK is to seek out and help UK exporters who wish to develop new opportunities in overseas markets.

Trade Partners UK's Gateway website at www.tradepartners.gov.uk is the focus for its services. The new website is simple to use and offers advice as well as information on overseas markets and connections to relevant services. Through it, users can tap into guidance from a world-wide network providing information, consultancy services and contacts. Services available overseas are described in more detail below. For companies who are not yet sure if they are ready to export, the Gateway provides a Self Assessment Checklist to help them gauge their potential. There are also links into the Trade UK sales lead service which, free of charge, provides UK companies who decide to register with sales leads from overseas. It also has facilities for overseas firms to check for UK sources of supply and to input their own sales leads.

As well as teams in London and overseas, Trade Partners UK has local international trade teams situated at Business Links throughout England, to give hands-on advice. Nine International Trade Directors have just been appointed, located mainly in the Regional Development Agencies, to co-ordinate this service. There are also networks operated by Scottish Trade International (STI), Wales Trade International and Trade International Northern Ireland (TINI).

Services to UK companies in the UK include:

- A special development programme to help new exporters prepare to work in overseas markets
- More than 100 Local Export Clubs, bringing newer and experienced exporters together. Meeting regularly throughout the year, they provide a forum for informal discussion on all matters relating to exporting
- Help in getting the language and cultural issues right, to ensure that companies make the most of the opportunities they identify

- Support to exhibit at the world's major trade fairs – and many less well known niche exhibitions
- Help to join other British companies on trade missions to major markets
- Special first time visit packages for new exporters to Europe, USA and Canada
- Other targeted activities to help put UK companies in touch with potential customers overseas.

Trade Partners UK Offices Overseas

Trade Partners UK is represented overseas by the Commercial Section of the local British Embassy, High Commission or Consulate. The Embassy's Commercial Section role is to develop and promote British trade overseas. Details of your local Commercial Section can be found at www.fco.gov.uk, choose the option 'UK Overseas Offices'. Commercial Sections offer various services to:

- British companies interested in commercial opportunities overseas
- Overseas companies looking for British suppliers and/or partners
- Overseas companies seeking investment opportunities in Britain.

Services to UK Companies

The Commercial team provides a wide range of advice and assistance to UK companies interested in exporting. Some of the services incur a charge, others are free. These include:

- Meeting a Commercial Officer
- Free 'off the shelf' market information
- Tailored Market Information Reports (incurs a charge)
- Promotional activity, focusing on priority sectors
- Provision of advance information on projects, tenders and market developments
- Conference, exhibition and office facilities (this varies depending on the facilities available locally)
- Advice on Commercial Publicity – New Products from Britain
- Arranging programme of visits to overseas companies (incurs a charge).

Services to Overseas Companies

The commercial team also provides expert and impartial advice and assistance to overseas businesses interested in locating products and/or services in Britain, representing UK companies and/or seeking partnerships with British companies. Please feel free to contact your nearest Commercial Section to arrange a meeting with the appropriate officer for your industry.

The Commercial Section can help you:

- Import from Britain
- Identify British sources of supply for specific products and services
- Become an agent/distributor for a British company
- Obtain information of forthcoming promotional events and trade shows in Britain
- Find Information on British participation at local international trade fairs
- Develop commercial/cultural British promotional events.

directory 78

Trade Partners UK
Kingsgate House
66–74 Victoria Street
London SW1E 6SW
www.tradepartners.gov.uk
The lead Government trade support service for
British companies trading in world markets.

Design Council
34 Bow Street
London WC2E 7DL
www.designcouncil.org.uk
Tel: 020 7420 5200
Fax: 020 7420 5300
Chief Executive: Andrew Summers
The Design Council is the UK's national authority
on design. It inspires and enables the use of
effective design on a strategic level by UK
business in the world context and also works to
raise design's profile within the education system.

Department of Trade and Industry
Design Policy Unit
www.dti.gov.uk/design
The Design Policy Unit's website provides
information on the UK design industry, useful
facts/figures and a directory of associated
organisations.

British Design & Art Direction (D&AD)
9 Graphite Square
Vauxhall Walk
London SE11 5EE
Tel: 020 7840 1111
Fax: 020 7840 0840
www.dandad.org
Director: David Kester
British Design & Art Direction (D&AD), founded in
1962, is a professional association and charity
working on behalf of the design and advertising
communities. Its remit is to set standards of
creative excellence, to promote this concept in
the business arena and to educate and inspire
the next creative generation.
Key Export Skills: setting creative standards and
promoting UK design and advertising excellence
internationally through its Awards Touring Show
and Annual Publication.

Design Business Association (DBA)
32–38 Saffron Hill
London EC1N 8FH
Tel: 020 7813 3123
Fax: 020 7813 3132
www.dba.org.uk
Chief Executive: Ian Rowland-Hill
The DBA is the design industry's trade association. Membership is open to consultancies
providing design services in all disciplines. In
1999 the association had a membership of 300
businesses, ranging from large multidiscipline
groups operating internationally, to small and
specialist groups. It is the largest design trade
association in the world. The DBA promotes
the effective use of design within business,
encourages high standards of business and
professional practice and provides a range of
services to member consultancies.
Key Export Skills: using world class companies to
open up new markets and clients through Trade
Partners UK-sponsored trade missions and
exhibitions, providing export training for up and
coming design companies.

British European Design Group
25 Stanmore Gardens, Richmond
Surrey TW9 2HN
Tel: 020 8940 7857
Fax: 020 8948 2673
www.bedg.org
Director: Karin-Beate Phillips
The British European Design Group (BEDG) is a collective of independent designers promoting their products in the international market place. BEDG was launched in 1991, when it staged an exhibition of UK creative design in the product sector.
Key Export Skills: organises international trade fair participation and overseas trade missions with British Trade International sponsorship, market research studies as well as curatorial work for exhibitions.

The British Council Design Department
11 Portland Place
London W1N 4EJ
Tel: 020 7389 3151/5
Fax: 020 7389 3164
www.britcoun.org
Head of Design Promotion: Emily Campbell
The British Council is working with Trade Partners UK, FCO and design partners in the UK, on a programme of activities to use British design skills to enhance perceptions of Britain as a forward looking, creative country. The Council organises high quality exhibitions, events and seminars.
Key Export Skills: market intelligence; access to key opinion formers, decision-makers and potential purchasers; increased awareness of British design service, thereby creating opportunities for British suppliers to do business.

The British Design Initiative Ltd (BDI)
2–4 Peterborough Mews
Parsons Green
London SW6 3BL
Tel: 020 7384 3435
Fax: 020 7371 5343
e-mail: initiative@britishdesign.co.uk
www.britishdesign.co.uk
Chief Executive: Maxine.J. Horn
Key Export Skills: Established in 1993, the BDI is dedicated to promoting the development of export business. It undertakes the following services:
Design Advisory & Recommendation Service – assisting overseas organisations seeking to invest in quality design consultancy to build export business.

Design Export News – a quarterly publication, which contains case studies and articles on the strengths of UK design and its export successes. It has a readership of over 20,000, 30% of which is overseas.
Design News Service – communicates with 3,000 press, radio and TV journalists, summarising the latest news on innovation, products and projects – material collected from subscriber design consultancies.
Design Export Register – records the products/projects designed by British designers for overseas companies. It is a resource available to British Trade International Export Desks to identify design strengths within their market in the planning of trade missions and market promotions.
BDI Website – houses a design directory with direct links to design consultancies' own sites. Attracting 500,000 visitors per year.
British Trade International sponsored trade missions, seminars, exhibitions and design workshops.
Capacity to undertake tailored export consultancy, market research and public relations campaigns.

The Crafts Council
44a Pentonville Road
Islington
London N1 9BY
Tel: 020 7278 7700
Fax: 020 7837 6891
www.craftscouncil.org.uk
Director of Sales Development: Karen Turner
The Crafts Council exists to promote and support the contemporary crafts and applied arts through exhibitions, training, education, advice, information and sales initiatives worldwide. More specifically it:
Organises major exhibitions at its London-based galleries.
Tours exhibitions of all scales throughout the UK.
Offers financial support to new designer/makers through its Setting Up Scheme.
Organises a range of seminars and conferences around all levels of education and professional development.
Offers advice and information services through its Library and Information Desk and promotes designer/makers through its digital image database Photostore.
Runs the Chelsea Crafts Fair.
Organises attendance at Trade, Gift and Art Fairs

in the USA, Europe and the Far East.
Sells directly through its shops at its London headquarters and at the V&A Museum.
Key Export Skills: Through its specifically designated unit for Sales Development, it offers expertise, advice and guidance to the sector. In addition, it maintains and develops a portfolio of trade and export initiatives in partnership with Trade Partners UK and The British Council.

Chartered Society of Designers (CSD)
32–38 Saffron Hill
London EC1 8FH
Tel: 020 7831 9777
Fax: 020 7831 6277
President: Lin Gibbon
Founded in 1930 it is the largest professional organisation of its kind in the world. It is dedicated to upholding the professional standards of the individual designer and the credibility of professional design. It tends to represent design professionals, design management consultants, sole traders or small consultancies in contrast to the Design Business Association, which represents business. Product and interior design are the predominant disciplines for CSD members, possibly due to the professional liabilities these carry with regard to health, safety and physical injuries.

Royal Society for the encouragement of Arts, Manufacturers and Commerce (RSA)
8 John Adam Street
London WC2N 6EZ
Tel: 020 7930 5115
Fax: 020 7839 5805
www.rsa.org.uk
Head of Design: Susan Hewer
The RSA, founded in 1754, is an instrument of change, working to create a civilised society based on a sustainable economy. It stimulates discussion, develops ideas and encourages action. Its main fields of interest today are business and industry, design and technology, education, the arts and the environment.

Published in 2001 by Laurence King Publishing
an imprint of Calmann & King Ltd
71 Great Russell Street
London WC1B 3BP
Tel: +44 020 7430 8850
Fax: +44 020 7430 8880
e-mail: enquiries@calmann-king.co.uk
www.laurence-king.com

Copyright © text 2001 David Redhead
© design 2001 SMITH
© studio photography 2001 SMITH
© concept 2001 id:uk

All rights reserved. No part of this publication may
be reproduced or transmitted in any form or by
any means, electronic or mechanical, including
photocopy, recording or any information storage
and retrieval system, without permission in writing
from the publisher.

A catalogue record for this book is available from
the British Library.

ISBN 1 85669 271 X

Printed in the UK